Here We Go Round
the Mulberry Bush

pictures by Roseanne Litzinge

HOUGHTON MIFFLIN COMPANY

BOSTON

ATLANTA   DALLAS   GENEVA, ILLINOIS   PALO ALTO   PRINCETON

Here we go round
the mulberry bush,
the mulberry bush,
the mulberry bush.

Here we go round
the mulberry bush
so early in the morning.

This is the way we
make our beds,
make our beds,
make our beds.

This is the way we
make our beds,
so early in the morning.

This is the way we
wash our clothes,
wash our clothes,
wash our clothes.

This is the way we
go to school
so early in the morning.

This is the way we
write our names,
write our names,
write our names.

This is the way we
write our names,
so early in the morning.

This is the way
we make new friends,
make new friends,
make new friends.

This is the way we
make new friends
so early in the morning.